THE GANGES DELTA
AND ITS PEOPLE

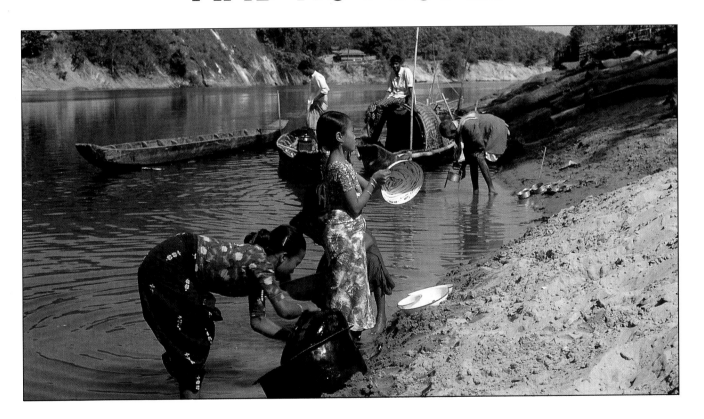

David Cumming

Wayland

PEOPLE
· AND PLACES ·

The Alps and their People

The Amazon Rainforest and its People

The Arctic and its People

The Ganges Delta and its People

Islands of the Pacific Rim and their People

The Mediterranean and its People

The Prairies and their People

The Sahara and its People

First published in 1994 by Wayland (Publishers) Ltd
61 Western Road, Hove, East Sussex BN3 1JD, England

© Copyright 1994 Wayland (Publishers) Ltd

British Library Cataloguing in Publication Data
Cumming, David
   Ganges Delta and Its People
   I. Title
   954.1

ISBN 0 7502 1146 6

Typeset by Dorchester Typesetting Group Ltd, England
Printed and bound in Italy by G. Canale & C.S.p.A.

Book editor: Katrina Maitland Smith
Series editor: Paul Mason
Designer: Mark Whitchurch
Consultant: Dr Tony Binns, Geography lecturer at Sussex University and Junior Vice-President of the Geographical Association

Acknowledgements

The publishers would like to thank the following for allowing their photographs to be reproduced in this book: Archiv für Kunst und Geschichte, Berlin 18, 19. Mary Evans Picture Library 20, 21 both. Eye Ubiquitous: (David Cumming) contents page, 12, 13, 35, 40; (L. Foroyce) 29, 32; (Jim Holmes/CAFOD) cover, 7 top, 10-11, 11 inset, 14, 15, 16 bottom, 23, 26, 27 both, 30, 31, 39, 41, 42, 43, 44, 45 bottom left; (TRIP) 7 bottom, 9, 25, 36-7. Ann & Bury Peerless title page, 4, 8, 17, 37 inset. Tony Stone Worldwide (Allan Bramley) 34.
Artwork by Peter Bull (5, 16 top, 22, 24, 38, 45 top right) and Tony Smith (6, 28, 33).

Cover: A man navigates his bicycle across the wide, green rice fields.

Title page: Few homes in the delta have running water, so washing-up has to be done in a river.

Contents page: In the delta, it is easier to travel about on water than on land.

C O N T E N T S

·THREE·RIVERS, ONE·MOUTH·

*F*rom its source high up in the Himalaya Mountains, the River Ganges travels 2,500km across northern India to the Bay of Bengal in the Indian Ocean. Just before reaching it, the Ganges meets the River Brahmaputra near the end of its own 2,900-km journey from southern Tibet, on the other side of the Himalayas. Further downstream they are joined by the River Meghna before their combined waters pour into the ocean through a maze of channels, both large and small. Only the Amazon carries more water into the sea.

The Meghna is hardly noticeable by the side of the other two giants of the Indian subcontinent. The Ganges and its tributaries drain 1,165,500km² of land; the Brahmaputra,

another 1,393,500km². Together they empty an area equivalent to three-quarters of the whole of India of all its water. This water contains a lot of sediment – at least two billion tonnes, which is more than in any other river system in the world. It is carried down to the shallow waters of the Bay of Bengal where it is dropped, forming the largest delta in the world. The delta covers an area of 130,000km² (the same size as Greece). Most of it is in Bangladesh, with only a small part in neighbouring West Bengal, a state in north-eastern India.

Every summer, melting snow and heavy rain fill the rivers with so much water that they burst their banks, turning central Bangladesh into an inland sea. Fierce storms

These boats carry jute to factories in Dhaka, the capital of Bangladesh.

Although it seems to occupy only a small part of the Indian sub-continent (below), the Ganges delta is a huge area which is the same size as Greece. The light-green area (right) shows West Bengal and Bangladesh

Area drained by the Ganges, Brahmaputra and Meghna rivers

blow in from the Bay of Bengal, pushing huge tidal waves in front of them which drown the coastal areas. Yet, in the winter months, there is a desperate shortage of water: the rivers shrink and the ground cracks as it dries out.

The Bangladeshis have to live with this cruel cycle of too much water followed by too little, and cope with it the best they can. They have no option. Although they have been fighting hard for years, the battle against nature has yet to be won – if it can ever be.

·N A T U R A L· ·F E A T U R E S·

*T*he delta owes its existence to the rivers flowing through it, for they have brought the land on which its people live and work. Millions of years ago, there was no Bangladesh, only ocean.

Because of the way in which it has been created, the land in a delta is very flat and low; more than 75 per cent of Bangladesh and neighbouring West Bengal is less than 10m above sea level.

Himalaya Mountains

Sediment is washed into rivers from mountains by melting snow and monsoon rains. Deforestation leaves soil unprotected.

Brahmaputra

Ganges

Tributaries also bring sediment.

Sediment is carried on to land during floods.

HOW THE DELTA IS FORMED

When it drains into a river, water – whether from rain or melted snow and ice – contains sediment. This is a mixture of mud, sand, earth and pieces of rocks and stones, picked up from the different types of land over which the water has passed. The current carries the sediment downstream to the river's mouth, where it is dropped as the water slows down on entering the ocean. The dropped sediment gradually builds up, layer on top of layer, to make the land of a delta.

Sediment forms new islands in mouths of rivers.

Bay of Bengal

Delta continues to grow as more sediment is brought by rivers.

The delta region is very flat and low, so villages are often flooded.

Huge banyan trees protect homes from the fierce sun and heavy rainstorms.

Not all of the sediment reaches the sea. Some is washed over the river banks during floods; some is deposited on the river bed, growing into islands which clog up the mouth. But much of it does get to the ocean and the Ganges delta continues to fan further out into the Bay of Bengal.

FORESTS AND WILD ANIMALS

About 10 per cent of the delta is covered in forests, most of them near the coast and on the hills along its northern edge. But even the plains in between are full of trees: every house and village seems to shelter in the shade of palm, mango or banyan trees – much needed in the summer months, when temperatures can soar above 35°C in the blazing midday heat.

In the hill forests, the leaves and branches of tall evergreen trees act like large umbrellas, shielding the soil beneath them from the heavy rain that can wash it away. This is one of the wettest parts of the world and a lot of rain can fall in a short time. In spring, the hillsides are dotted with the colourful flowers of magnolia, rhododendron and camellia.

On the western edge of the delta and overlapping into West Bengal is the Sundarbans: an enormous soggy swamp of some fifty muddy islands covered with tropical forest and separated by hundreds of channels and creeks. Much of it is submerged by the sea at high tides, and the trees and plants have adapted to spending half their lives standing in salty water. Many have developed long, trailing roots' to anchor them in the mud. Others have roots that breathe, called pneumatophores. These are spiky tubes that poke up through the mud, taking in air while the tide is out.

Many animals live in the Sundarbans, including Royal Bengal tigers, crocodiles, monkeys, deer, monitor lizards and wild boars. Among the bird life, there are herons, cranes, storks and snipe.

In the delta as a whole, there are some 300 species of birds. The best known are the mynah, which the local people often train to talk, the brilliant-blue kingfisher and the fishing eagle.

Bangladesh is also home to a variety of animals, both large and small. The hills are the haunt of ponderous elephants, cheetahs, leopards and panthers; the plains, the gecko lizard and that fearless hunter of snakes, the mongoose. Many types of river and sea fish can be found in the water, along with flesh-eating turtles and crocodiles.

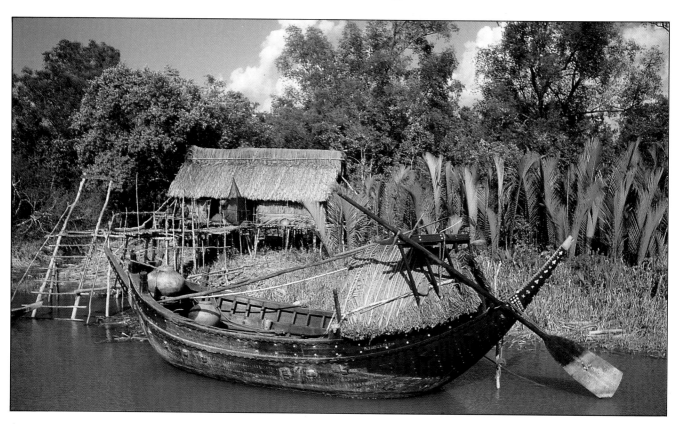

A home in the forests of the Sundarbans in West Bengal.

An increasingly rare sight today: a Royal Bengal tiger.

Hunters have nearly wiped out the Royal Bengal tiger. A national park has been set up in the Sundarbans in West Bengal to protect the remaining population, now numbering fewer than 300. Royal Bengals grow to over 3m long and 1m in height, and weigh up to 250kg. This is the only member of the tiger family to live in swamps, where it retreated after its natural habitat, the forests on the plains of West Bengal and Bangladesh, was destroyed by settlers. The tiger has altered its behaviour accordingly, becoming equally at home in water – swimming up to 10km between islands – as on muddy land where it thunders along at 24kmh in pursuit of prey. It will eat fish or meat and drink fresh or salty water.

In old age, and losing teeth and energy, Royal Bengals turn to easier prey: some of them turn to humans. Each year, about thirty people are the victims of these elderly man-eaters. The local people try to kill them using clay human dummies wired to batteries which they leave in the forests. Any tiger that attacks one of these dummies is electrocuted. Since it is a protected species, the local people are only allowed to trap those Royal Bengals that are man-eaters. All others must be left alone, by law. This, however, has not stopped poachers hunting the tigers for their bones. Indian businesspeople sell the bones to China, where they are used in traditional medicines for the treatment of arthritis.

· R I C H · L A N D · POOR · PEOPLE ·

*T*he delta's land is excellent for farming. It is very flat and the soil is rich. The hot, wet climate means a lot of rice can be grown – so much that the Bangladeshis call their country *sonar Bangla* (golden Bengal) because of the colour of the rice when it is ripening in all the fields. Today Bangladesh is the fourth largest rice producer in the world. Yet millions of Bangladeshis are poor and suffer from illnesses caused by having too little to eat.

VILLAGE PEOPLE

There are few towns and cities in the delta, but thousands of villages. In Bangladesh alone there are 70,000 villages, in which 80 per cent of the population lives.

In the countryside, there are no factories providing jobs, so people can only work on the land. They grow crops to eat, but also to sell so that they have money to buy the things they need. In Bangladesh, owning a piece of land is as important as having a job in countries which are mostly industrial.

A major problem in Bangladesh is that a small number of rich people own a lot of land, while millions of others have either very little or none at all. The landowners make up 10 per cent of the population, but they own 60 per cent of the land. They provide work for the people without land, either by letting them farm the land in return for a share of the harvest, or by employing them for a wage when help is needed – with gathering the crops, for example. Many of the landowners treat their employees badly, often paying them low wages or offering

them an unfair share of the harvest. While the landowners become richer, their employees usually get poorer.

Besides the large landowners, about 30 per cent of the population owns land, but only a small amount. Religion is the main reason for their farms being small. About 85 per cent of Bangladeshis are Muslims, the followers of Islam. According to Islam's inheritance laws, fathers have to split their land when they die. All the children are entitled to a share of their father's land, though the daughters receive less than the sons. Farms that were once large have been broken up again and again over the generations,

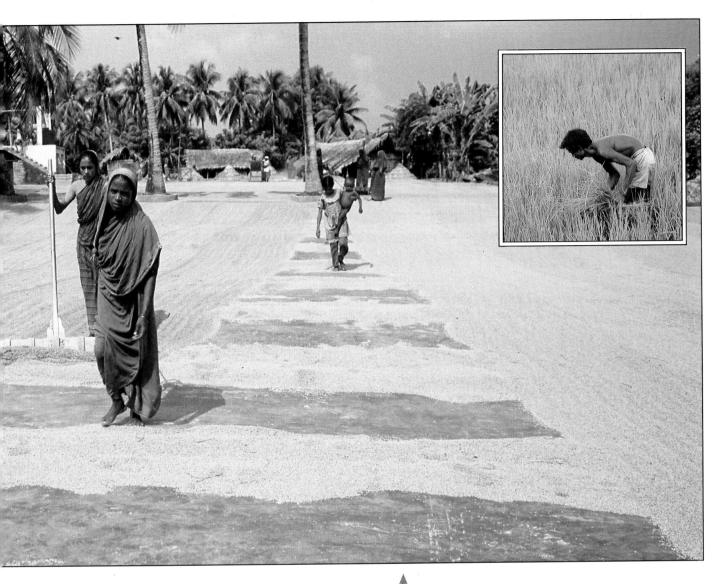

becoming smaller and smaller. Today, 90 per cent of farms are less than 3.5ha. This is just enough land for a family to grow sufficient food to eat, but there is little to spare for growing crops to sell.

In a bad year, when the harvest is small, a farmer might have to buy extra food for his family. To do this, he will have to borrow money from the local moneylender. This person is usually a rich landowner who will charge the farmer a high rate of interest on the money he lends. If the farmer fails to pay back the money, the landowner can take his precious land and the farmer ends up working for him. In return, the farmer will receive

▲

After harvesting, the ripened rice is dried in the sun, usually in the main square of the local village. Inset: Rice growing in a paddy field.

some of the food he needs for his family, but he will also need to buy food in the markets. These are often controlled by the landowner who can keep food in store so that prices rise and he earns more money. So the poor go hungry, while the landowner gets richer. For many people, life in the country becomes too much of a struggle and they leave for a city such as Calcutta or Dhaka, hoping that it will be easier there.

The biggest city in the delta is Calcutta, in West Bengal. Like many others in the developing world, it is already at bursting point, yet its population of 12 million increases daily. The new arrivals are usually young men trying to escape the tough life of a farmer. Calcutta has many factories, but they already have enough workers. Most of the men from the country end up scratching a living doing odd jobs here and there. Housing is just as scarce. If they are lucky, the new arrivals will find a home in a crowded slum. Life here is unpleasant, but it is better than joining the half a million people living on the pavements. Either way, whether in a slum or on the pavements, they will be flooded out in the monsoon and stand a high chance of catching a dangerous disease, like cholera, from the dirty water.

▶

In Calcutta, the pavements are home to thousands of families. Many have come to the city from the countryside, in search of a better life.

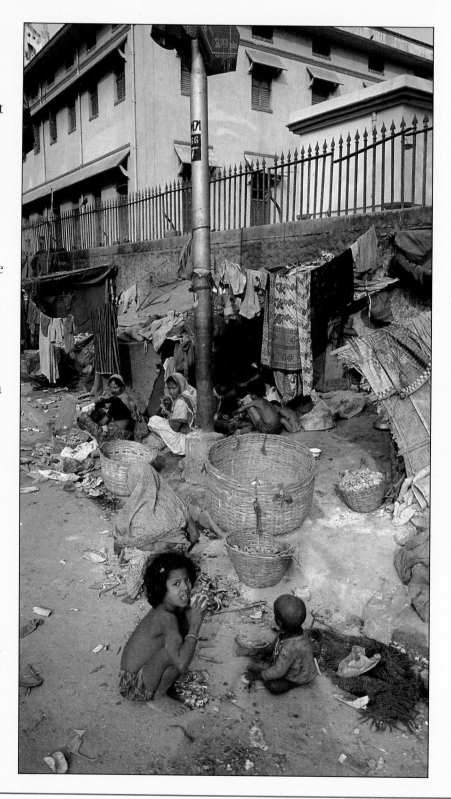

Cholera: the World at Risk

◄ *These men do not have water in their homes in Calcutta, so they have to wash at a pump on the street instead.*

'In April 1993 we dealt with 22,000 people with cholera. We had to put them four to a bed and on the floors of the corridors. I have never seen so much suffering.' This was how Dr B.K. Das of the Infectious Diseases Hospital in Calcutta described the start of a cholera epidemic which may spread to many other countries, killing hundreds of thousands of people.

Cholera is a deadly disease of poor countries where sanitation is usually bad. It is caused by poisonous bacteria found in water containing raw sewage. Unless they are treated quickly, adults die within nine hours and children within six hours. Cholera is common in the delta because the waste from thousands of villages drains directly into the rivers. The rivers are used for washing and drinking water by millions of people every day.

Cholera has existed in the delta since the fourth century. In the present century, six epidemics have started there. The one that began in 1993 could be the worst yet. The cholera is a new type and existing vaccinations do not stop people catching it. Thousands have already died in West Bengal and Bangladesh and many more will die from the disease, both there and abroad. A cargo of Bangladeshi seafood which was shipped to Japan was found to contain cholera – fortunately, the discovery was made before any of the seafood was sold in the shops.

TOO MANY HUNGRY MOUTHS

Bangladesh is one of the most crowded countries in the world. Only a little larger than England and Wales, it is home to nearly twice as many people: 115 million in all. Roughly 1,300 people live in every square kilometre, sometimes even more.

Earlier this century, Bangladeshis did not expect to live long. Few reached old age, and many died young. So, even though many babies were born, the population increased slowly. Today better hospitals and more doctors mean that more people are living longer. There is still a high number of babies being born, so the population of Bangladesh is growing every year by about 3 per cent, or 3.5 million people.

Working on the land involves a lot of time and effort, and crops can be ruined by the weather. With no money for machines, Bangladeshi farmers have to rely on their family for help. The more children in a family, the more hands there are available to work the land, and the higher the chances are of there being one or two who can support the others through the bad times.

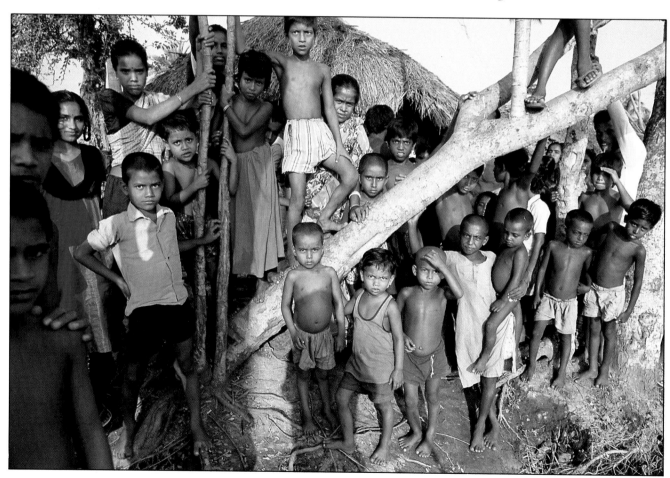

▲
Children in Batbera village. Most Bangladeshi children work instead of going to school.

This Bangladeshi mother is teaching herself to read: she was not sent to school when she was young.

Even though there are now more hospitals and doctors to treat illnesses, many Bangladeshi babies still die. One baby in ten does not reach its first birthday, and one in four will die before it is five years old. Out of every 100 babies, 60 will be in poor health because they do not have enough to eat. When they are weak, babies cannot fight off diseases, so they die very easily. Parents have many children in the hope that several will survive childhood and live long enough to look after them in their old age.

There is very little birth control or family planning in Bangladesh because of the pressures to have many children and because parents are unaware of the problems created by large families. Never having been to school, most of them can neither read nor write. Education is seen as a waste of time when a child can be out earning a living or helping on the farm.

Of the children who are sent to school, there are more boys than girls. As a result, only 19 per cent of women can read and write, compared to 30 per cent of men. This puts men in a more powerful position than women. In a Muslim country, like Bangla-desh, women are meant to stay at home to look after the family. Because they are not expected to get jobs, it is not thought necessary to send girls to school. Instead, they learn about running a home from their mothers. A daughter will copy her mother's behaviour in the home, doing the things she has always done.

Boys are influenced by their father's behaviour. In a Muslim country, men make almost all the decisions, frequently without consulting their wives. Most men want large families just to prove their manliness. Today 45 per cent of Bangladesh's population is under 15 years old. If these children copy their parents, the population will expand faster than it is doing at present. Unless there are fewer babies born each year, the population of Bangladesh will double by 2023.

There are already too many people in Bangladesh. Most of them are farmers with small farms. If families remain large, the farms will become very much smaller as they are split up when the father dies. The number of people without land will increase. People will remain poor and continue to have too little to eat.

The Farming Year

Rice likes a wet soil in which to grow, so most of Bangladesh's rice is grown during the main rainy or *aman* season. The rice is sown in June or July, just before the heavy monsoon rains, and is harvested after they have finished, in November or December. However, if the floods are very bad, much of the *aman* crop may be ruined. Many farmers also grow an *aus* crop, planted in March or April just before the 'little rains' which come before the monsoon. This is harvested in July or August. If a farmer can irrigate his land, he is able to grow a third crop of rice, the *boro*, during the dry winter from November to April.

This farmer can irrigate his land, so he is planting boro *rice in the winter.*

Most of Bangladesh's rice is grown during the wet summer months.

A farmer using a hollowed-out tree trunk to scoop water out of a river. He cannot afford a machine to pump it on to his rice fields.

INCREASING FOOD PRODUCTION

In a good year, there is just enough food in Bangladesh to feed everyone. But farmers are finding it difficult to grow any more than they do at the moment. Soon there will be too many mouths for them to feed.

The main food grown in Bangladesh is rice. About 60 per cent of it is grown during the wet, or *aman*, season of heavy monsoon rains. Most farmers plant a second rice crop before the 'little rains' which precede the monsoon. A third crop can be grown over the dry winter if a farmer can irrigate his land to make up for the lack of rain.

At present only 25 per cent of the land is irrigated enough for it to be used in winter. If this area could be increased, farmers could grow more food all year round. They could grow even more food if they planted this land with modern high-yielding varieties of rice, which can produce six times the harvest of traditional types. The new varieties do not thrive in deep water, so they would be of no use in the *aman* season when floods are common. Irrigation would also help during the rare summers in which the monsoon fails and too little rain falls.

The problem with both these ways of increasing the amount of food grown is their price. Not only are high-yielding seeds more expensive to buy than traditional varieties, they also require more chemical fertilizers and pesticides while they are growing. Tube wells and diesel pumps for irrigation are even costlier. Bangladeshi farmers have hardly enough to live on, so finding money for new equipment is very difficult. Although rich landowners have the money, they are usually not interested in trying to increase the quantity of crops grown on their farms. Many of them live in towns far away from their land and spend most of their time looking after their other businesses, which earn them more money.

·THE·DELTA· ·IN·HISTORY·

A late-sixteenth-century Indian
illustration shows a new palace being
built for Akbar the First. Such buildings
showed the wealth of the Mogul empire.

The Dravidians were the first known inhabitants of India. Small and dark-skinned, they survived by hunting, and gathering berries and plants in the forests. Originally from the dusty, dry Deccan plateau in central India, the Dravidians moved on to the plains by the side of the River Ganges, where water was plentiful and the rich soil better for growing crops. One group, the Bangas, headed north-east, ending up in the delta. Here they established a kingdom, first called Banga and then Bangala.

In about 1500 BC the Aryans from Central Asia arrived in north-west India and spread across the northern plains, following the route of the Ganges. Tall and fair, they thought the Dravidians inferior and treated them cruelly. The Bangas, however, seem to have impressed the Aryans when they conquered the delta. Instead of fleeing for their lives, the Bangas adopted the Aryans' way of life and converted to one of the two Aryan religions, Hinduism and Buddhism.

The Aryans were toppled by the Moguls, another people from Central Asia, who attacked India in AD 1526. By the end of the century their greatest emperor, Akbar, ruled an empire stretching across the whole of northern India as far as Bangala. By then Bangala had become the richest Aryan kingdom, having grown wealthy through trading its rice, silk and saltpetre. Under the Moguls, it continued to prosper: trade increased, and new cities were built with impressive forts, palaces and mosques. Local writers, painters and artisans were all encouraged to produce new works to show off their talents and culture. Most of the population converted to Islam, the religion of their new rulers.

The East India Company had to protect itself from attacks from both land and sea. This is the company's Fort St. George on India's south-eastern coast.

EUROPEAN TRADERS ARRIVE

By the time the Moguls seized power, the sea route from Europe to India had been discovered by the Portuguese navigator, Vasco da Gama. Companies from Britain, France and The Netherlands began competing fiercely with each other to trade with Bengal, as Bangala was renamed. From its headquarters in Calcutta, the British East India Company was the most important.

As the Mogul empire broke up, the East India Company expanded into other parts of India and employed an army to protect itself from jealous rivals. After the Indian rebellions of 1857, known as the Indian Mutiny, the last Mogul emperor left India and the East India Company was left in control of most of the country. The British government immediately took over all the Company's activities and began to rule India itself.

THE DELTA IN BRITISH TIMES

The British made many changes during their time in Bengal. One of the most important was the introduction of a tax on land. To earn money to pay their taxes, farmers were forced to grow what the British wanted to buy. What the British wanted most of all was jute, not the rice most of the farmers cultivated. So farmers began growing more jute in their fields and less rice. After harvesting, the jute was taken to factories in Dhaka and Calcutta to be turned into ropes, sacks and material for carpet backs, before being sent to Britain. Under the British, farmers in the delta began using more of the land for growing crops to sell than for growing food.

Industry, too, altered under British rule. Before they arrived there were many mills in Dhaka where cotton from the hills in the north was woven into textiles for clothes. The mills were closed down by the British because they took business away from the textile factories opened in Britain during the Industrial Revolution. Cotton was still allowed to be farmed, but was taken directly to Britain. Some of the clothes made there were then brought back to Bengal to sell to its people.

The British were only interested in making improvements that benefited them rather than the delta's people. True, they built roads, railways and river steamers, but these were to make it easier for the jute and cotton to be brought from the countryside to the factories and docks. Local people were also specially trained to work in offices and factories. Again, this was not to help them, but to make sure that everything worked smoothly for the British companies.

During British rule, Calcutta became the most important city in Bengal and, indeed, in the whole of India. India was governed from there, and it was also the main centre for business and culture. The rest of Bengal developed in its shadow, including the other major city, Dhaka.

Huge sacks of raw cotton ready to be shipped back to textile factories in Britain in 1870.

◄ Calcutta in 1895 – the capital of British India.

The cover of an Italian weekly paper of 1947 illustrates the awful fighting that followed India's independence.
▼

LA DOMENICA DEL CORRIERE

Supplemento settimanale illustrato del NUOVO CORRIERE DELLA SERA - Abbonamenti: Italia, anno L. 930, sem. L. 500, - Estero, anno L. 1530, sem. L. 800

Anno 49 — N. 38   21 Settembre 1947   L. 20 (Arretrati L. 30)

India senza pace. Nella città di Nuova Delhi turbe fanatiche di Indù hanno fatto irruzione nel quartiere musulmano sgozzando uomini donne e bambini, saccheggiando e appiccando incendi. Diecimila persone sono cadute nello spaventoso massacro. (Disegno di W. Molino)

INDEPENDENCE FROM BRITISH RULE

At the start of this century, many Indian politicians felt that the British were doing more harm than good to their country. They decided it was time for the British to leave so that they could look after their own affairs. The people supported the politicians and the British became so unpopular that they had no choice but to let India become independent in 1947.

At that time, the two largest religions in India were Hinduism and Islam, which had survived since the Aryans and Moguls. In India as a whole, most people were followers of Hinduism. However, in the north-west and north-east, there were more Muslims than Hindus. When India became independent, these areas became Pakistan, a new country split in two by 2,500km of northern India. In the north-west was West Pakistan. In the north-east, in what had once been eastern Bengal, there was now East Pakistan.

The struggle for independence had been a bloody one. The Indians had fought the British, as well as each other, Hindu against Muslim. Pakistan had been created to keep the two religions separate. What no one anticipated was that the people of Pakistan would start fighting one another.

Key

■ The Indian province of West Bengal since 1947

□ East Pakistan from 1947 to 1971; Bangladesh since 1971

■ West Pakistan from 1947; now known as Pakistan

This map shows how India was split up after the British left.

BANGLADESH: LAND OF THE BANGLAS

In the same way that the Indians came to dislike the British, so the East Pakistanis soon grew angry with the way the West Pakistanis treated them. West Pakistan was richer than East Pakistan in every way. Its industries were better, as were its schools, roads and hospitals. When Bengal had been split in 1947, the richer western half remained part of India and became the Indian state of West Bengal. The poorer eastern half of Bengal became East Pakistan. West Bengal had almost all the factories but little farming land. East Pakistan was left with most of the farming land but very few factories. East Pakistan had also lost many skilled people because they were mainly Hindus who had left to live in India.

Instead of helping East Pakistan to build new factories and train people with skills, West Pakistan did everything to stop its progress. It did not share its wealth with East Pakistan and much of the money that was earned by the East was taken and used by West Pakistan.

In 1971, East Pakistan rebelled against West Pakistan and broke away to form the new state of Bangladesh (*desh* is the local word for land and the name, Bangladesh, means 'land of the Banglas'). After nearly twenty-five years of being treated badly by West Pakistan, Bangladesh was one of the poorest countries in the world. Life has changed little since then. Bangladesh has few factories. Its most important ones are connected with agriculture, processing the crops farmers grow in their fields. With few factories, the people have no choice but to work on the land, hoping that it will provide them with food and money. In Bangladesh, therefore, both the factories and the people depend on farming. All over the world, farmers are affected by the weather, but those effects are particularly dramatic in the Ganges delta where months of too much water are followed by months of too little.

·FLOODS·

*B*ecause the delta is very flat and low, it floods easily during the heavy monsoon rains in the summer. In a good year, only 20 per cent of the land will be flooded; in a bad year as much as 80 per cent. In the last century, there were 6 bad years; in this one, 14 so far. The floods in 1988 were the worst for a long time: 66,000 villages were under water, making 45 million people homeless, and at least 2,000 people drowned. The floodwater comes from three sources: the rain, the rivers and the sea.

RAIN AND FLOODS

About 1,800mm of rain falls every year on the delta. Most of it – about 80 per cent – is brought by the monsoon winds that blow in from the Bay of Bengal from June right through to October. So much rain falls in these five months that all of the water cannot drain through the ground. The ground of the delta is like a giant sponge. It soaks up the rain until it can hold no more and a deepening layer of water begins to settle on top.

▲
A school stranded by rivers flooding after the monsoon.

RIVERS AND FLOODS

The amount of water carried by the rivers flowing into the delta determines how deep will be the layer of floodwater during the rainy season. The rivers bring more than four times the water brought by the monsoon. The monsoon rains arrive when the Ganges and Brahmaputra are at their fullest, swollen with the melted snow and ice from the Himalaya Mountains. The rainwater raises their levels to the point where they either brim over or burst through their banks, adding more water to a land already flooded by rain. The River Ganges' drainage basin is south of the Himalayas, while the River Brahmaputra's is to the north, so they normally reach their fullest at different times, a month or so apart. However, in some years they are full at the same time and then the flooding in the delta is much worse.

Most of Bangladesh is flooded every summer, much of it beneath several metres of water. The areas of light green on the map show land that is least likely to flood.

Wave of Destruction

'The wind was more than 180kmh, pushing a tidal wave over 9m high. It came at night, as they often do, sweeping people away while they slept. Here we must fight the sea to live.' These are the words of Rafiqullah Chowdhury, a government official on Sandwip Island, recalling the tidal wave that swept across it in November 1970, killing 40,000 people. Along the rest of the delta's coast 300,000 people and 500,000 cattle died; one million were left homeless; 70 per cent of Bangladesh's fishing boats were wrecked and 80 per cent of the rice crop lost.

▲ *This large ship was sunk by the super-cyclone that struck Bangladesh in 1991.*

THE SEA AND FLOODS

As the inland areas begin to dry out in the autumn, it is the turn of the coast to be drowned. It is hit by cyclones. These are fierce tropical storms which form over the Bay of Bengal. In other parts of the world they are known as hurricanes (in the Caribbean Sea and Pacific Ocean) and typhoons (in the China Seas). The direction in which the cyclones head is unpredictable. In some years, southern India suffers; in other years the delta is the victim. When this happens, the hurricane-force winds of the cyclones push water up into the north of the Bay of Bengal. The narrower and shallower the bay gets, the higher the water is forced, until it builds into a wave up to four metres high, which is often topped by other waves just as tall. The resulting huge wave roars over the islands and lowlands at the delta's mouth, sweeping away anything in its path. Later, it retreats, dragging everything it has destroyed into the Bay of Bengal.

In the past 32 years, Bangladesh has been hit by 16 cyclones. All of them have caused enormous destruction, but the one that struck in 1991 was one of the most terrible ever. It has been described as a 'super' cyclone, with winds more powerful than even the biggest atom bomb. The winds, and the huge wave they created, killed 139,000 people and made 10 million homeless.

·LIVING·WITH· FLOODS·AND· CYCLONES·

After the terrible floods of 1988, a specialist from the United Nations Development Agency visited Bangladesh to see how they could be prevented. He decided that floods brought more benefits than harm, and that it would be wrong to try to stop them altogether.

NO FLOODS, NO FARMING

Without floods, farming in the delta would be more difficult. As plants grow, they remove all the soil's beneficial nutrients. In most countries these are artificially replaced with fertilizers. However, in Bangladesh, fertilizers are not necessary. On their journey downstream, the smaller particles of sediment in a river are ground down, forming a fine soil called alluvium. This is full of all the nutrients plants thrive on. When a river floods, the alluvium is spread over the surrounding land, leaving a layer of rich soil after the floodwaters drop. Every year, the rivers fertilize the delta's soil – for free.

If the flooding were halted, the delta's farmers would have to buy chemical fertilizers, or their fields would soon lack the goodness plants need. Not only are fertilizers very costly for people with little money but, when the rain washes them off the land, they pollute the rivers. In solving one problem, fertilizers would create another.

This Bangladeshi family cannot leave home because of rising floodwaters.

Fishermen in Danger

If flooding is stopped, the land will need fertilizers. These will add to the chemicals already being used by farmers to control pests, diseases and weeds in their fields. Water from the fields now pollutes the nearby lakes, ponds and swamps from which Bangladesh gets 90 per cent of its fish. More chemicals will increase the chances of harming the fish, and the people who eat them. Some five million people earn a living from fishing. Already they have lost money because ponds have been drained for more fields. Chemicals may now also lose them their jobs. The population as a whole will be affected since fish provides it with most of its protein, an essential part of any diet.

◄

Chemical pesticides are used on tea plantations in north Bangladesh. In the delta, such chemicals can harm fish.

▼

FLOODS: A PART OF LIFE

In most of the world, floods are seen as one of the natural hazards people have to cope with only occasionally. In Bangladesh, they happen every year. Floods come with the rainy season; next year will be the same, and the year after that. The only thing people cannot predict is how bad the floods will be. Everyone agrees that they are a nuisance and destructive, but they also realize that without floods there would be nothing to eat. For centuries, people have continued to live in the delta, aware of the danger, but willing to accept the risk.

In 1988, the delta's three main rivers, the Ganges, Brahmaputra and Meghna, reached their fullest within a few days of each other. At the point where they all meet, there was so much fast-flowing water that sections of river bank a hundred metres wide were eaten away. The River Meghna was so powerful, it changed course, opening up a new channel twenty metres wide. Land, homes, railways, people and cattle disappeared in a few hours. Everyone was unprepared because they had been given no warning, and many people lost everything. Nearly 70 per cent of

The Changing Landscape

Before the Monsoon

The land of the delta is very flat and covered with the fields of small farms where rice is the main crop (1). Villages are built on the highest ground (2) in the hope that it will protect them from the floods. They are connected by tracks raised above floodwater level on embankments (3).

The Monsoon Season

During the heavy rains of the monsoon, the rivers swell and flood the land (4). Sometimes a river will form a new channel (5) and create further islands (6). If they are built on land that is high enough, the villages remain above the level of the floodwater, but the floods can wash away parts of embankments (7).

After the Monsoon

As the land dries out, the changes to the land brought by the monsoon are seen. Sediment left by the floodwaters may extend islands (8) and cut off sections of river, leaving lakes filled with fish (9). Although crops may have been ruined, the alluvium spread over the land during the flooding will act as a rich fertilizer. Damaged embankments must now be repaired (10).

A village of bamboo houses is built on stilts to keep it above the floodwaters.

Bangladesh was flooded, much of it beneath several metres of water. The capital city, Dhaka, did not escape. Its streets were awash and people had to walk to work through knee-deep water. The sewers overflowed, sending dirty water and sewage onto the streets and into houses. In the countryside, farmers watched helplessly as their crops were washed away.

When the water subsided, people returned to daily life. The next harvest was one of the best for a long time.

Floods are part of life in the delta, so the people have developed ways of living with them. In areas where flooding is particularly bad, farmers grow a special type of rice with a very long stem. The grains at the top of the stem are held above the floodwater to be ripened by the sun.

Riverside houses are often built on stilts to keep them clear of danger in the monsoon. In the countryside, villages and homes are on the highest ground, connected by tracks along embankments above floodwater level. For most farmers a small boat is more useful than a cart. In the summer they can take short cuts across drowned land; in the winter there is enough water in the maze of narrow channels for them to paddle to market. People are more accustomed to travelling on water than on land, and there are no bridges and few roads and railways in a region where there is almost as much water as land. The rivers and their tributaries are the delta's highways, bustling with boats laden with farm produce being rowed or hauled; crowded, lopsided ferries; battered, elderly paddle-steamers and rusty coasters.

Concrete cyclone shelters like this one can save thousands of lives.

LIVING WITH CYCLONES

The islands on the delta's coast are affected the most by cyclones. Many people live there because the soil is good for farming rice and growing coconuts, tomatoes, peppers and vegetables such as radishes and cauliflowers. There are also many fishermen, who catch the shrimps living in the Bay of Bengal's shallow waters. The fishermen's homes are simple huts made from mud or coconut matting, with straw or coconut leaves on the roofs. They are easily blown away by a cyclone's winds, and easily rebuilt. The islands are low so, when the tidal waves come, there is no high ground for people to escape to. To avoid being washed away, many climb to the tops of the coconut trees and tie themselves to the trunks. The cyclones bend the trees, but they rarely break. The tidal waves flood the land with salty sea water which makes it impossible to farm until the water has drained away. For many months the people have little to eat.

Many islands now have buildings made of concrete which are strong enough to withstand high winds and tall tidal waves. The buildings are large enough to hold 3,000 people and they are often equipped with medicines and food. On one island, everyone was killed by a cyclone in 1970. Afterwards, the government constructed a concrete building in which people sheltered during a cyclone in 1991. Everyone survived.

There are 300 concrete buildings on the delta's islands, but 3,000 more are needed. The government of Bangladesh cannot afford more. Each one costs about $120,000. Until these extra shelters are made, thousands more people will lose their lives in the cyclone season.

Floods cause Famine too

Most of us associate famine with a lack of rain, but this is not always the cause. After the floods of 1974, 300,000 Bangladeshis died of starvation. A shortage of money rather than food led to their deaths. Most were landless labourers who had lost their jobs because the land was under water. They could no longer afford to eat. Their plight was made worse by the government cutting back low-priced food for the poor by 70 per cent. Its stocks were low because the USA had stopped sending food aid, annoyed with Bangladesh for trading with Cuba against its wishes.

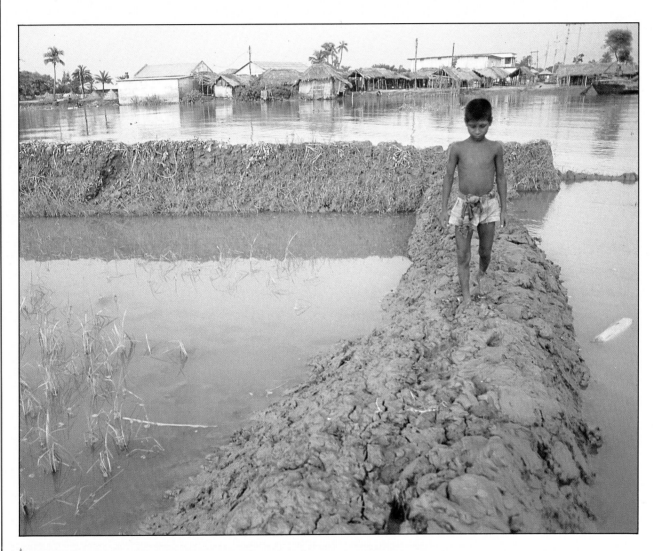

Farmers cannot work the land when it is flooded, and many lose their jobs. Building mud embankments around rice fields can protect the land and crops from floods.

· P R E V E N T I N G · F L O O D S ·

Everyone understands that it is difficult to control two huge rivers like the Ganges and Brahmaputra. Many people wonder if it is worth trying: with over 57,000 cubic metres of water rushing past every second in the monsoon, they consider the rivers too powerful to tame. Nevertheless, the government of Bangladesh, helped by other countries, is trying to reduce the damage done by floods.

Since the 1960s, river banks have been raised and strengthened with concrete. However, large parts of central Bangladesh remain at risk from deep floods. In 1991 work began on the Flood Action Plan. When it is completed, thousands of kilometres of land alongside the Ganges and the Brahmaputra will be much safer because strong, high banks will have been built.

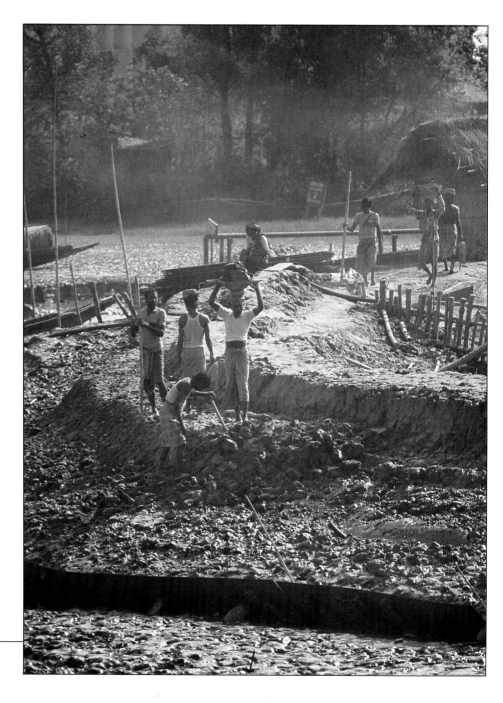

These people are strengthening river embankments in Bangladesh to prevent them being washed away by floods.

Himalaya Mountains

Planting more trees on hillsides helps to stop soil being washed away by rain.

Water behind dam across Brahmaputra can be released into delta in dry season.

Brahmaputra

Canal linking Ganges and Brahmaputra diverts water away from delta.

Dam across Ganges controls flow of water to delta and generates hydro-electric power.

Ganges

Canal takes water from Ganges to irrigate southern India.

Less water reaches delta in summer, preventing floods. Less sediment is brought to block rivers and mouth of delta.

▲
Help from Bangladesh's neighbours could lessen flood damage in the delta.

Some people criticize the Flood Action Plan. They think that it will create bigger problems nearer the coast. All the water that once flooded central Bangladesh will now flood the coast, they say. So while one area has fewer floods, another will have worse ones. The critics also point out that more water going down to the delta's mouth will increase the chances of a catastrophe similar to the one that happened in the 1970 monsoon. Then, the water rushing down the rivers reached the mouth at the same time as a huge tidal wave came in from the Bay of Bengal and 500,000 people drowned.

NEIGHBOURLY HELP

The countries drained by the Ganges and Brahmaputra can help prevent Bangladesh's floods. If these countries built dams and canals, the amount of water reaching Bangladesh could be controlled. Less river water arriving in the monsoon season would make the flooding less serious.

The Brahmaputra comes from southern Tibet. Tibet is governed by China and, at the moment, China does not want to help. The River Ganges starts in India, and India is willing to assist Bangladesh with its flood problems. India is investigating the possibility of linking the Brahmaputra and Ganges by a canal. The Ganges would also be connected to a 3,000-km canal network to irrigate the dry lands of central and southern India. The combined projects would divert water away from the delta in the monsoon. It is a very ambitious idea, and would take at least thirty years to complete if the money could be found for it.

Deforestation in Nepal

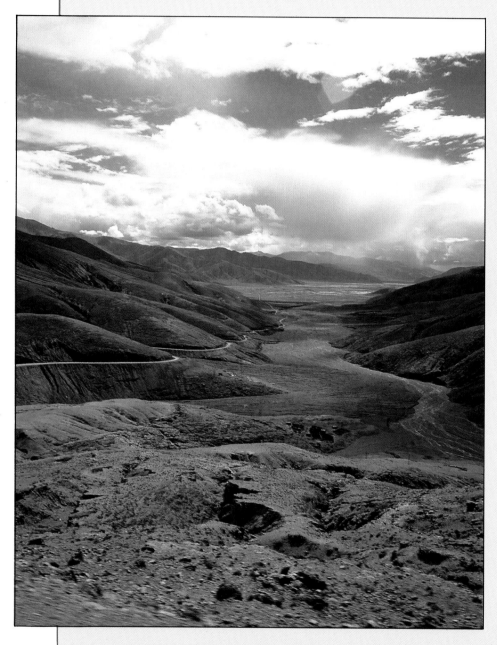

In the last fifty years, 30 per cent of Nepal's hillside forests have been cut down. Today 500km² are lost each year, while only 80km² are replanted. Without trees to shield the ground from the heavy monsoon rain, huge quantities of soil are being swept into the rivers and down to the delta, making floods even worse. India, too, must accept some of the responsibility, for it has been destroying as much of its own forests. The situation is made worse by the nature of the Himalayas. They are very young mountains, so they are still 'soft' and easily worn away by the wind and the rain, adding more sediment to the rivers flowing down them.

◄

__Deforestation of the Himalayas in places like Tibet (pictured) and Nepal allows rain to wash soil into the rivers.__

Nepal, whose rivers drain into both the Ganges and the Brahmaputra, can also help. Another poor country like Bangladesh, Nepal's population has been growing so quickly that it has been cutting down forests at an alarming rate to obtain fuel, building materials and farming land. An increasing amount of soil is now being washed from the land into the rivers. This ends up on the river beds in Bangladesh, making the channels shallower. They can carry less water, so they flood more easily.

COASTAL FLOODING

Protecting the coast from being flooded by the sea is even more difficult than preventing rivers flooding inland. Banks are the only way of keeping the sea out. Not only must they be high enough to block tidal waves, but also tough enough to cope with the very strong winds caused by cyclones. Such barriers are very expensive. Many people argue that it would be better to concentrate on measures that would directly protect people rather than worrying about land and property being ruined by sea water and wind.

One way of protecting the coastal people is to build more of the concrete shelters mentioned earlier (see page 30). Communications would also need to be improved so that the people are given sufficient warning of a cyclone to have plenty of time to reach a shelter. Weather satellites regularly fly over the Bay of Bengal and transmit reports back to Dhaka. Radar stations have also been built which can watch a cyclone's progress. The satellites and radar provide enough information for scientists to predict accurately how bad a cyclone is, where it will hit the coast and when it will arrive. Although officials in Dhaka know what is happening, it is very difficult to pass this information on to the people in the path of the storm because they do not have radios, televisions or telephones. Many meteorologists are worried that cyclones will become even more destructive in years to come. If communications within Bangladesh can be improved, thousands of unnecessary deaths will be prevented.

High earth embankments can stop rivers flooding villages in the Sundarbans.

·DROUGHTS·

*I*n the summer, the delta people have to cope with too much water. In the winter, they have to live with too little. The situation is made worse by sea water entering many of the rivers and channels.

THE DYING WESTERN DELTA

The rivers in the delta often alter course. Normally it is only a minor shift, such as cutting a corner when a build-up of sediment blocks the main stream. At other times, it can be a major change in direction brought about by tremors or upheavals in the earth's crust. A severe earthquake in 1787 made the Brahmaputra turn south to join the Ganges (although a tributary still follows the old route, connecting it to the Meghna). Long before that, in the twelfth century, the delta's land had tilted, forcing the Ganges to flow into the Bay of Bengal through Bangladesh. Previously it had travelled down what is now the River Hooghly in West Bengal, reaching the sea to the south of Calcutta.

The delta in West Bengal and western Bangladesh has been drying out ever since the Ganges changed course. Its tributaries there have become choked with sediment and weeds, with insufficient water in them to prevent salty sea water being pushed further and further inland by the powerful tides. Watered only by the rain, the soil has lost its fertility, while the amount of salt in it has increased. It badly needs a river's nutrients to enable plants to grow in it again.

The Ganges–Kobadak irrigation scheme was designed to bring life back to the dying delta in western Bangladesh. Water pumped from the Ganges through a network of canals and channels would be used on 90,000ha of

dry and infertile land. The project was started in the 1950s and was nearly finished when the Indian government built the Farakka Dam to the north, robbing it of the water it needed. The western delta remains dangerously close to turning into a salty desert. In parts of it, the level of salt in the soil is as much as thirteen times greater than before the Farakka Dam was opened.

PUMPS AND TUBE WELLS

Across the delta, farmers have to sink tube wells deep into the ground or draw water up from the rivers with diesel-engine pumps. Few farmers can afford them. As a result, only 25 per cent of the land is irrigated sufficiently to grow crops during the dry winter season – a huge waste when there are so many mouths waiting to be fed.

In winter, when there is no rain, the ground cracks in the western delta through lack of water. Inset: Sinking a tube well to an underground reservoir can provide water to stop the ground cracking and allow crops to be grown.

Farakka Dam adds to Bangladesh's Problems

'If salt levels continue to rise at present levels, then the western delta risks turning into a desert. Soon nothing will grow there,' warned a Bangladeshi geographer recently, pointing an accusing finger at India's Farakka Dam. Opened in 1975, the dam was built to flush sediment out of the River Hooghly by diverting water from the Ganges. Less water now flows down the Ganges into Bangladesh, so more salt water penetrates further into the delta. This harms crops and fisheries, as well as people's drinking water. The Indian government has promised to help by building a canal to transfer water from the Brahmaputra to the Ganges.

Key
- Limit of salt water before dam built
- Limit of salt water after dam built

▲ *India's Farakka Dam has increased the amount of salt water in the delta.*

Even if farmers have the money for wells and pumps, the water can do more harm than good because it contains a lot of salt. Though the problem is most serious in the western area, it is widespread across the delta. The reason for it is the same: during the dry season there is less water in the rivers so more sea water is able to push its way inland, some of it reaching the underground reservoirs of fresh water. By taking water from the rivers and reservoirs, farmers make the situation worse, because they are making room for yet more sea water.

There are two ways of stopping the sea water. The simplest method involves building mini-dams with sluice-gates along the coast. During the heavy rains of the monsoon, the gates are left open to let the water out. In winter, they are shut, keeping the sea out of the delta and preventing fresh river water from escaping.

Alternatively, if dams were built on the Ganges and Brahmaputra, water held back in the summer to reduce flooding could be released in winter to fill the rivers and force the tides back.

·THE·WAY·FORWARD·

Before it became independent in 1971, Bangladesh was part of British India and then Pakistan. The British were only interested in what was grown in Bangladesh. They made the farmers grow a lot of jute because it was wanted by industries in Britain, and most of the factories they built were for preparing the jute before transporting it. The other factories built by the British were also for processing crops, like tea and cotton, ready for sending home. When Bangladesh was part of Pakistan, little changed because West Pakistan did not want East Pakistan to have industries that might rival its own.

As a result, Bangladesh has only a few small industries to make the things, such as machines, which it needs. Much has to be bought from abroad. To earn money for this, Bangladesh has to sell what it produces to other countries. Since jute has become its major crop, it is the most important thing the country can sell – in the past, nearly 60 per cent of the money Bangladesh earned came from jute. Jute used to be very valuable as the only material suitable for making sacks and ropes. Now, more and more artificial materials are used, so Bangladesh cannot earn as much from jute. Cotton clothes, fish, leather and tea are also sold abroad, but they bring the country little money because these industries are so underdeveloped in Bangladesh.

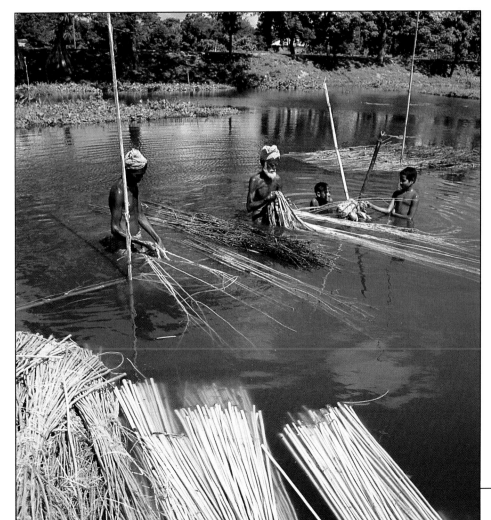

After harvesting, jute is soaked in water before being taken to a factory for processing. The fall in the value of jute, Bangladesh's main export crop, means that the country has to find other ways to earn money.

The money Bangladesh earns from other countries is used both to buy the things it needs and to build new factories. Bangladesh has to spend most of the money on buying things which means little is left over for factories. Because there is so little money to develop new and existing industries, the people of Bangladesh have to remain farmers. They must use the land not only to provide them with food but also as the only way they, and the country as a whole, can earn money. How much food and money they get depends on the weather. This can destroy all the farmers' crops, leaving them with nothing and Bangladesh with no produce to sell to other countries.

Bangladesh needs more factories. These would provide people with alternative jobs and industries to farming. Less would have to be bought from abroad and more things could be sold to other countries. The extra money earned could be used to build more factories, as well as new hospitals, homes, schools, roads and railways. With more factories, Bangladesh could become a richer country which is better equipped to look after its people. Without help from other countries, it will be very difficult for Bangladesh to get richer.

FOREIGN AID

The help given to a poor country by a richer one is referred to as aid. It can take many forms. If the help comes only from one country, this is known as bilateral aid; from several countries acting together, multilateral aid. Help after a disaster, such as a cyclone, is emergency aid and, if only food is sent, it is called food aid. The provision of money for a particular scheme, like building river embankments to reduce flooding, is project aid. If the money can only be used to buy goods and services from the helping country, it is known as tied aid.

Bangladesh receives all these types of aid every year. For example, it gets about three million tonnes of food aid; more if there has been heavy flooding or severe cyclones. This is in addition to the $5 billion in money, a mixture of project and tied aid, sent by governments and international organizations like the United Nations and the World Bank.

HOW FOREIGN AID CAN HELP BANGLADESH

Richer countries can provide Bangladesh with money and machines for new factories. Businesspeople and experts can provide advice on the best way of running them.

In agriculture, foreign aid can help farmers grow more food. Increased irrigation in the winter will allow more land to be used for rice and for other food crops like wheat. The channels dug to bring the water to the fields will also act as drains in the summer monsoon, controlling where the water flows to prevent floods ruining the harvest. Motor-powered pumps and tube wells are also needed, but few farmers can afford them. High-yielding varieties of rice are costly too, both to buy and to raise, since they require more chemicals than traditional types. If they were used, farmers could produce bigger harvests without increasing the size of their farms. The chemicals used to grow these varieties, however, can cause pollution problems, especially for the local fishermen.

More factories like this steelworks in Calcutta are needed to give people jobs away from the land.

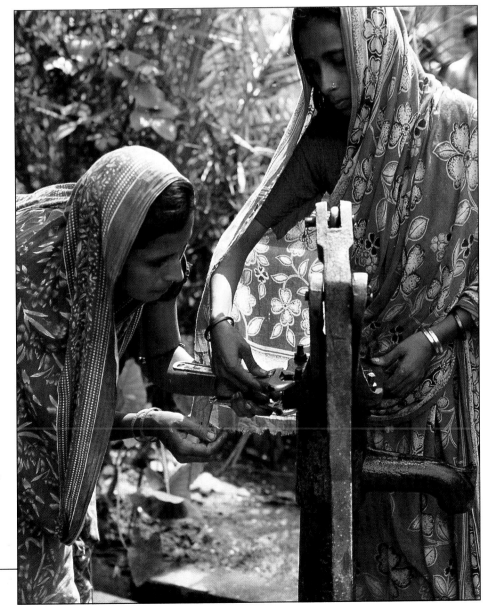

These Bangladeshi women have been trained to take care of tube wells in their village.

Other countries can assist the Bangladeshi government in expanding the banking system so that more branches are opened in the countryside to help farmers and villagers. They can be given loans at low interest, either to buy equipment for their farms or to open small businesses such as workshops to make and repair farm equipment. The high interest rates charged by local moneylenders make this difficult at the moment.

The government can also be helped to train health and social workers who can be sent out to villages to give advice on family planning, diet and hygiene. Given the opportunity, women can do a lot to change Bangladesh. At the moment men make almost all the decisions in towns, villages and within families. Social workers can set up women's groups where women can discuss things and be encouraged to give their opinions more openly. The groups can run reading and writing courses, as well as passing on skills that will enable women to practise a craft to earn money.

Communications throughout Bangladesh need to be improved so that goods and people can travel around more easily and warnings of cyclones can be given more effectively. More roads need to be built and the railway system modernized.

Bangladeshi mothers learn about water-borne diseases.

Does the West always know best?

Two buildings in one: this cyclone shelter is also a school.

Critics of foreign aid often attack Western governments and institutions for wasting their money on huge construction projects when it could have been better spent on simpler and more effective solutions. They point to the World Bank's Flood Action Plan in the delta as an example of money being wasted. The World Bank is spending $5 billion to improve embankments along the Ganges and Brahmaputra Rivers to reduce flooding – a massive undertaking. Many people think that it would have been better to build well-equipped community shelters on high ground and to improve communications to give earlier flood warnings. This would have been cheaper and would have saved as many lives.

Bangladeshi villagers learn about government savings schemes that will help them buy farming equipment.

IS FOREIGN AID THE BEST WAY?

Many people say that foreign aid does not help a poor country like Bangladesh. They say that the richer countries often do not ask the poorer countries what they most need. As a result, a lot of money is often wasted building something that is of little use.

Any loans of money have to be paid back. If a poor country cannot repay its loans, it builds up debts, which get bigger and bigger each year. Soon it is borrowing money just to pay off the interest on the debts. Instead of becoming richer, the poor country becomes even poorer.

Tied aid, too, can harm poor countries because they are forced to buy things such as machinery from the country from which the aid comes. This machinery may not be of the type needed. It may also break down a lot and require expensive spare parts. While these may be cheaper elsewhere, a poor country is forced to buy them from the supplier of the aid.

Some of the money loaned to Bangladesh is also 'tied' to the wishes of the governments or organizations providing it. If they disap-prove of the Bangladeshi government's behaviour or plans, they will often stop the aid or reduce it in the following year. The US government, for example, assists Bangladesh on condition that it does not trade with certain countries. When it found out that Bangladesh was selling things to the Communist state of Cuba, the US sent less food aid.

Much of the aid given to Bangladesh never reaches the people and places for which it is intended. Corrupt government officials spend the money on themselves and the people who vote for them. Many businesspeople steal machinery for their own factories. Others take food aid to sell in markets.

Despite all the problems connected with foreign aid, without help from abroad Bangladesh will be unable to break free from the circle of poverty in which it is trapped. It has many problems because it is a poor country, and because it is poor it can do nothing about them. Without aid, it will always remain poor and the problems will continue. Foreign aid is helping Bangladesh to help itself. Eventually, Bangladesh will be rich enough not to need outside help.

Fish Island benefits from Foreign Aid

Although frequently criticized, foreign aid can be useful. One example is Meendwip (Fish Island), 100km south of Calcutta, in the Hooghly estuary on the Indian side of the delta. The World Bank is making a loan of $50 million to the government of West Bengal to turn it into the biggest prawn farm in India, providing jobs for 12,000 people. Some 2,500 fishermen's co-operatives will be based there. Cold-storage and processing plants will be built to prepare the prawns for export, which will earn India millions of dollars of much-needed foreign currency. Some of this will be used to develop parts of the island for tourism, bringing even more jobs to an area currently with none. Without aid, Fish Island would remain in its present deserted state.

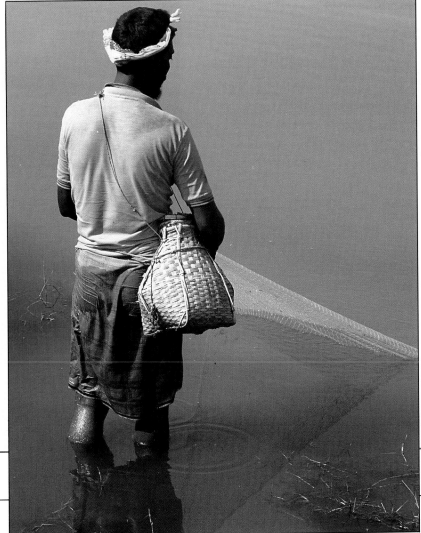

Meendwip (Fish Island) was formed from the sediment brought by the Ganges when, centuries ago, it flowed down what is now the River Hooghly. The area is rich in seafood.

This prawn fisherman belongs to one of the co-operatives on Meendwip which will benefit from the island's development.

GLOSSARY

Alluvium The fine, fertile soil that is left on the land after flooding.

Banyan tree An Indian fig tree with branches that hang down and root themselves in the ground.

Communist state A country in which the wealth produced by industry and agriculture is meant to benefit everybody in the country.

Deforestation The removal of trees over a large area, usually to provide land, fuel or building materials.

Delta An area of land, usually fan-shaped, formed by the build-up of sediment at the mouth of a river.

Drainage basin The area of land from which a river and its tributaries receive all their water.

Drought A long period without rain or with only a very small rainfall. It may last for months, often years.

Endangered species A particular type of animal that is at risk of dying out.

Fertile When describing soil, it means it is good for farming, since crops will grow easily in it.

Fertilizer Nutrients added to the soil to keep or make it fertile. It usually describes chemicals, although there are also natural fertilizers, like animal dung.

Independence A country gains independence when it breaks away from being ruled by another country.

Interest Money which is paid for the use of a loan.

Irrigation Supplying water to farming land, often by building canals and ditches.

Jute A plant of East India. Its golden-coloured fibres are used to make sacks, ropes and carpet backs.

Meteorologist A person who studies the weather.

Mogul The Arabic and Persian word for Mongol, which was used to describe the family of Indian emperors started by Babur (1483–1530). He claimed to be the grandson of Genghis Khan (1162–1227).

Monsoon Summer winds from the Indian Ocean that bring rain to much of India and Bangladesh. The word is also used to describe the main rainy season.

Nutrients Minerals needed by plants to grow.

Pesticides Chemicals used to kill insects harmful to plants.

Reservoir A large lake where water is stored:

underground reservoirs occur naturally beneath the earth's surface.

River system A large river and all the tributaries flowing into it. When two or more large rivers combine, as in the Ganges delta, the term describes all the rivers involved.

Saltpetre A salty substance used in gunpowder.

Sediment Small particles of earth and rock picked up from the land and carried by rivers until they are dropped when the flow of water slows down.

Sluice-gate A sliding gate that controls the amount of water flowing through it.

Subcontinent A large area of land smaller than a continent.

Tremors (or earth tremors) Very small earthquakes.

Tributaries Rivers or streams that flow into larger rivers.

Tube well A pipe driven into underground water reservoirs, with a pump at the top to draw up water.

World Bank The International Bank for Reconstruction and Development, set up to lend money to countries to encourage development.

BOOKS·TO·READ

Anu in Bangladesh by Naila Kabeer & Olivia
    Bennett (A & C Black 1988)
Flood by Julia Waterlow (Wayland 1992)
The Ganges by David Cumming (Wayland
    1993)
Pakistan and Bangladesh by Graham
    Houghton & Julia Wakefield (Macmillan
    1989)
Pakistan and Bangladesh by Nicholas
    Nugent (Heinemann 1992)

More advanced readers will find the following books interesting:
Chasing the Monsoon by Alexander Frater
    (Penguin 1991)

Slowly Down the Ganges by Eric Newby
    (Picador 1976)
A Walk Along the Ganges by Dennison
    Berwick (Century 1986)

Two books containing good photographs
are:
The Ganges by Raghubir Singh (Thames &
    Hudson 1992)
A Journey Down the Ganges by Mukul &
    Saith Kesavan (Lustre Press 1989)

·USEFUL·ADDRESSES·

Action Aid
Old Church House
Church Steps
Frome
Somerset BA11 1PL

Council for Environmental Education
School of Education
University of Reading
London Road
Reading RG1 5AQ

Friends of the Earth (Australia)
PO Box A474
Sydney NSW 2001

Friends of the Earth (New Zealand)
PO Box 5599
Wellesley Street
Auckland West

Friends of the Earth (UK)
26–28 Underwood Street
London N1 7JQ

WWF (World Wide Fund for Nature) Australia
Level 17
St Martin's Tower
Sydney NSW 2001

WWF New Zealand
PO Box 6237
Wellington

WWF UK
Panda House
Weyside Park
Godalming
Surrey GU7 1XR